Best wishes

Allan Miller

Orrell
in old picture postcards

by Dr. Allan Miller

European Library   ZALTBOMMEL/THE NETHERLANDS

GB ISBN 90 288 2617 3

© 2000 European Library – Zaltbommel/The Netherlands

European Library
post office box 49
NL – 5300 AA Zaltbommel/The Netherlands
telephone: +31 418 513144
fax: +31 418 515515
e-mail:publisher@eurobib.nl

Introduction

Located four miles west of Wigan, Orrell always had two distinct centres. One was at Orrell Post where the road from Ormskirk to Wigan crossed the road leading northwards from St. Helens to Standish. The other was to the south-west at Far Moor, which developed around the point where the St. Helens to Standish road was crossed by minor roads running west to east at the four 'Lane Ends'. To the south, Orrell's 'bare and treeless' landscape merged into the colliery district around Billinge. At the eastern extremity was Lamberhead Green, which was 'as sunk in besotted ignorance as Far Moor'. To the west, Orrell was divided from Up Holland by the Dean Brook that flowed through a 'pleasantly wooded dingle' to join the River Douglas, which formed the northern boundary at Gathurst. The northern part of Orrell at least was 'pleasantly situated upon the banks of the Douglas'.

The traditional economic activities of Orrell were farming, coal mining and nail making. In the manufacture of the nails, little hammers were used and Orrell was referred to as the 'Land of the Little Ommers' and the villagers were known by the nickname of 'little Ommers'. Orrell was transformed by the Industrial Revolution, which saw improvements in transport and the development of cotton mills and brick works. This expansion of economic activities was matched by a rise in Orrell's population from 1,883 in 1801 to 6,773 in 1921. Life was hard for villagers with unemployment, poverty and disease never far away.

The Catholic and Protestant churches in Orrell responded to the changes and challenges unleashed by the Industrial Revolution. Extensive building programmes were launched to provide churches and Sunday schools, which prior to the establishment of day schools provided children and adults with free basic education and moral instruction. The churches were also social centres designed as a counter attraction to the plethora of public houses in Orrell. This is covered by Adrian Alker in his excellent booklet 'Faith and Fellowship at Far Moor'.

Orrell people also benefited from the developments in local government. On 21 June 1872 a meeting of the ratepayers of the Township of Orrell at the National School in Far Moor agreed to implement the Local Government Act of 1858 by appointing a Local Board of twelve members with Mr. W.H. Harbuttle, Managing Director of Orrell colliery, appointed as its first Chairman. After the Local Government Act of 1894 Orrell was governed by an Urban District Council of twelve members. The first meeting of the new Council took place on 31 December 1894 and Dr. Robert Hartley became the first Chairman.

The main sources of information on Orrell are scattered and my research took me as far afield as the Bodleian Library in Oxford. The Minutes of meetings of the Orrell Local Board and the Orrell Urban District Council are deposited in the Lancashire Record Office at Preston and the Minutes of meetings of Wigan Urban District Council are located at Wigan History Shop. These give the local government perspective from about 1870. It is interesting to compare the official line with things that were happening on the ground in Orrell as recorded in the Wigan Observer and the Wigan Examiner, which are preserved on microfilm at the Wigan History Shop. I have also explored the archives at Leigh Town Hall, St. Joseph's College in Up Holland, the Independent Methodist Resource Centre in Lamberhead Green, Manchester Central Reference Library and local university libraries. Records of individual churches, school logbooks and the various trade and commercial directories are mines of information.

The book is dedicated to Mr. Harry Parkes, who adopted Orrell as his home base and for over fifty years photographed the Wigan area. His pictures provided a fascinating record of the social and economic life in the Wigan area and without them this book would not have been possible. Unfortunately, most of Mr. Parkes's original negatives, photographs, postcards and slides have been destroyed. However, I am obliged to present members of the family for permission to use copies of his pictures in this book. Many of Harry Parkes' photographs were published in the Wigan Observer and, thanks to the efforts of my friend, Peter Williams, copies of these photographs have been made from the microfilm of the newspaper. I am grateful to Mr. A. Wareing, Director and General Manager of Lancashire Publications Limited, for permission to make these copies from the Wigan Observer. I am also indebted to the Wigan Heritage Service for permission to use photographs from their archives and from the microfilms. The picture of an Orrell coal mine (Number 27) was provided by Lancashire Mining Museum and Tony France. The family of the late Ralph Worthington made his scrapbooks available to me. Many other people, too many to mention by name, provided me with photographs and information.

1   This picture shows the crossroads at Orrell Post with the historic beech tree in front of the Stag Inn. The Orrell Local Board met in the ivy-covered terraced houses and dealt with a range of work and problems. In 1887 Mr. W. Holt applied to set up a slaughter house in Sefton Road and Mr. Peet wished to erect a wooden stable on the site of the old gravel pit also in Sefton Road. In 1888 the fence around the pit pond in Moor Road belonging to the Thomas Evans brick works was in a very dangerous condition. Local Board workmen cleared the pond and legal action was threatened against anybody throwing dead animals into the pond and thereby causing 'a nuisance injurious to health'. In the same year a cow, killed in the slaughter house set up in the stables at Abbey Lakes, was suspected of being diseased and the meat unfit for human consumption. The Medical Officer found the cow's lungs to be in a bad condition and the flesh very poor. However, a butcher declared the meat fit for sale!

Orrell Post, Orrell, Wigan

2 The first meeting of the Orrell Local Board had taken place on 31 July 1872 in the Assembly Room of Orrell Gardens, which were owned by 'Old William Nickson'. Mr. Nickson was elected to the Board but resigned to become the Surveyor of Highways and Nuisance Inspector at a salary of £30 per annum. The actual gardens contained flower beds and fruit orchards; the south wall was heated by coal burning grates and was covered for 60 yards with vines. Orrell Gardens continued to be an important assembly point for locals and for visitors. A number of rooms were open to the public. During the 1890s technical instruction classes were held at Orrell Gardens. Local people could enrol for elementary classes in mathematics, bookkeeping and commercial correspondence, drawing (freehand and geometrical), handwriting, shorthand (elementary and advanced), cookery, dressmaking and cutting. The hall was also used as a place of worship by the Christadelphians before it was demolished in 1936.

3 According to Whellan's Directory of 1853 'a neat stone pillar, of considerable antiquity, called Orrell Post, stands in the township' and this most distinguished landmark still stands outside the Stag Inn at Orrell Post. The substantial stone column dated back to 1750; the date stone was cut into the stone at the base of the pillar with the initials 'T.N.' just above it. The big stone ball on top of the historic landmark represented the world. It was used as a distance post in horse and foot races. The soldier on crutches was Private Melling who lost a leg in the First World War. In January 1880 the 'ordinarily quiet little village' was disturbed by 'extra ordinary, riotous scenes' around the Stag Inn. Mrs. Margaret Der-byshire claimed to have legal documents to the Orrell Estate, which had been in the possession of the Leigh family for more than a century. The Estate consisted of land and properties, including cottages, the Stag public house and the Red Lion beer house.

4 Mrs. Derbyshire and her supporters occupied a cottage at Orrell Post, one announcing 'his intention of inflicting condign punishment on anyone who dared to molest him'. They faced police charges that they 'unlawfully and riotously did assemble to disturb the public peace, and they did make a great riot and disturbance to the terror and alarm' of the area. The Derbyshires continued to push the case and informed tenants that 'land and premises on the Orrell Estate ... are now claimed as being our absolute property ... and all rents must be paid to us'. They occupied Latham House and declared: 'We, the true and lawful owners of the Orrell Estate, do hereby take possession according to law, which does say that possession is a good title against all but the true owners; so that being the Derbyshire family they do challenge any person or persons to come forward and dispute our claim who can do so.' In 1912, the courts found for the Leigh family and Orrell Post returned to its 'normal aspect'.

5   Orrell Hall was once the home of the Leigh family whose battle with the Derbyshires was immortalized in 'The Siege of Orrelle Poste' by James Gaskell:

And thou, Orrelle, our own Orrelle,
shalt live in hist'ry's page,
For heroes yet unborn shall tell
how fierce thy war did wage,
How humble Derbyshire defied the
haughty house of Leigh,
How all the countryside around
came forth the joust to see.

'Twas on a Thursday morning in
the first month of the year,
That all the strength of Derbyshire
at Orrell did appear,
Forthwith they sped with eager
steps unto the place of siege,
And Ev'ry knight, in armour
bright, vowed fealty to his liege.

And came they from the Abbey
lakes and Holland fair to see,
And all the yeomen true who liv'd
on this good propertie.
They bound themselves by solemn
oath that ere they slept that night
They would regain the citadel or
perish in the fight;

And this their battle cry was rais'd
mid that determin'd host,
Long live our gracious Lord of
Leigh and Henry of the Poste.

6 This picture from November 1934 shows work in progress on the demolition of the old Red Lion Inn, another of Orrell Post's historic landmarks. The site was being cleared for the development of business premises. In the old days publicans used to brew their own ale; the brewing house of the Red Lion was subsequently converted into a cottage. During the 1870s the Red Lion was owned by the Albion Brewery Company, which was contacted by Orrell Local Board because the state of the buildings at Orrell Post was presenting dangers to passengers, children and to occupiers of adjacent properties. The Red Lion and the Stag were resorted to by the supporters of the Derbyshire family during their protracted dispute with the Leigh family:

This night high wassail we will keep, to celebrate this day,
And Derbyshire right royally will all his friends repay.

Let trusty messengers in haste for English ale be sped,
And drain the cellars of the Stag, likewise the Lion Red.

7 Another distinctive landmark on the Orrell Post scene for many years was the wooden hut that was Mr. Orrell's newsagent shop, which was located next to the Stag Inn. In addition to newspapers, the cabin prominently displayed advertisements for cigarettes and tobacco. When Mr. Orrell moved across the road to new permanent premises, the hut became an electrical store. To its rear another wooden building was occupied by Rogerson's bicycle, and later motorcycle, business. The hut was a prominent landmark at Orrell Post until it was demolished when the road was widened to cope with increased traffic and to improve safety. The road junction at Orrell Post had a long history of traffic accidents. In September 1884 a horse and cart were in collision with a lamppost, the cart overturned and the driver was killed. In January 1935 the dangerous junction was improved by the introduction of white lines and 'automatic Robot signals'.

8   Orrell Post could be a particularly hazardous place in winter. Bad weather in 1920 produced a great deal of damage in the Wigan area and Orrell did not escape. In October a storm washed away the bridge leading from Spring Road to Gathurst, leaving the road in a very dangerous state. A severe storm in December 1920 caused havoc throughout the Wigan area, with chimney pots blown off, shop windows shattered and roads and tramways blocked by falling trees. The giant beech tree, which had stood for years at Orrell Post and was one of the best known landmarks for miles around, was blown over by the violent gale. It could have been a major tragedy, because the old tree crashed on to the very spot where the regular 12.30 p.m. motor bus to Billinge had loaded up with passengers only a short time before the tree toppled.

Fall of the Big Tree Orrell Post Dec 9th 1920

9 The villagers of Orrell Post turned out in force to pay their last respects to the old stricken beech tree. The loss of the beech tree was like saying goodbye to an old friend, because it had acted as a focal point and an open air forum for local people. There were many sad faces at the post mortem, even the sawyers whose task it was to dissect the old tree seemed to be unhappy. The bearded man in the centre of the picture was old Ned Baldwin. The Baldwin family was one of the oldest in Orrell. They owned and worked coal mines around Orrell Post and the terraced houses opposite the Stag Inn were known as 'Baldwin's Terrace'. The sawyer was George Hook and to the left of Ned Baldwin in the picture was Jem Molyneux, who used to keep the old Red Lion public house at Orrell Post.

10   By the early years of the 20th century it was obvious that Orrell needed a new Council Office. The elegant design of the new Orrell Urban District Council Office was the work of Mr. R. Pennington, a Wigan architect. The foundation stone was laid by Mr. C. Hartley, Chairman of the Council, on 19 June 1907 and the office was opened in March 1908. Located at one end of Orrell Gardens, the site and the building cost £1,500. The trade in Orrell 'had improved wonderfully during the last ten years' and Orrell was becoming 'quite a residential district' with 'steady and regular growth' of population, and 'every year having seen a number of new houses built'. The work of the Orrell Urban District Council had expanded as a consequence, so that the old offices in the terrace at Orrell Post were totally inadequate for the growing variety of work of local government. Overcrowding was the major problem; sixteen people met together in what was ordinarily a bedroom and hence the need for new premises.

11 The front entrance of the new Council Office opened into a spacious hall that ran right through the building, and from which a staircase led to the upper floor, and a staircase down to the basement. The ground floor consisted of a boardroom and offices for the Clerk, Sanitary Inspector and Collector. The whole of the upper floor was laid out in one room, which could be divided for evening classes and other purposes. In the yard were workshops, storerooms and a room that could be used as a public mortuary. In July 1933, County Coroner criticized the mortuary: 'I don't call it a mortuary in any shape or form. It has none of the proper appliances for a medical man to conduct a post mortem examination, and it is now occupied by the corpse and a large quantity of disinfectant. How people can honestly think this is reverence to the dead I can't imagine.'

12 Whellen's Directory of 1853 described Orrell Hall, 'a mansion in the Elizabethan style of architecture', as a 'large farm house' that was the property of Sir Robert Holt Leigh, 'the principal landowner in the township'. The Hall in Spring Road was an important and attractive social centre, especially in spring when its grounds were covered by daffodils. In September 1930, the occupants, Major and Mrs. Taberner, organized an American Tea in aid of Up Holland Village Infant School. Spring Road itself was one of the local beauty spots. There was 'hardly a prettier district' with footpaths to Dean Wood and Porter's Wood with their brooks rambling to the River Douglas at Gathurst. Holiday makers on foot and travelling past in cars gazed at the 'arches of climbing roses bearing thousands of blooms' over the doorways and windows of the 'five picturesque stone cottages' on the crest of the hill in Spring Road.

13 Worrall's Directory of 1881 listed no less than 23 farmers; as this picture showed, one of the most picturesque farms was Orrell Mount Farm where peas were 'grown by the acre'. The Victoria County History of Lancashire described Orrell as a 'fertile township' whose soils were 'clay with a mixture of sand over a foundation of hard stone'. The country round about was 'open and varied' and consisted of 'pasture land and fields' and the crops were 'chiefly potatoes, wheat, and oats'. A quaint local custom enabled a new tenant farmer to call on his neighbours to give him a day's ploughing free of charge in return for providing his helpers with 'bagging' (food). Cooperation was needed in 1881 when a fire at Orrell Hall Farm virtually destroyed the farm buildings, which were used to store hay, straw and corn and as stables and shippons. Wigan Fire Brigade could not be called upon because Orrell Local Board had refused to make a financial contribution to the cost of the Fire Brigade.

14 Blacksmiths were important craftsmen in the village, especially in the era before mechanization when the numbers of horses used in agriculture and for transport were significant. Trade directories in the middle of the 19th century listed William Dean, William Gaskell, William Quayle, William Brown and Thomas Martlew as blacksmiths. Thomas Makinson was a blacksmith, wheelwright and agricultural implement maker and the family occupied the smithy at Orrell Post, shoeing horses, making and repairing wheels, making and sharpening scythes, sickles and shears.

In 1909, John Makinson, apprentice to his father, took into the smithy an orphaned piglet from an Up Holland farm. He nursed it through the winter by the smithy fire, giving it milk and food from a spoon. It followed the blacksmith like a dog and became quite a local attraction. Eventually it was placed in a sty beside the smithy door and the blacksmiths were able to concentrate on their services to the people of Orrell.

15 In 1810 John Clarke, banker and coal mine owner, purchased the 'Orrell Post Estate' and built Orrell Mount. French Benedictine nuns occupied the site from 1821 until 1835. The 'Benedictine Dames' taught young ladies every branch of useful knowledge 'becoming the delicacy of their sex', including French, English, Italian, writing, arithmetic, geography, history, embroidery, needlework, music and drawing. 'By their unremitting and successful attention to the education of the youth of the catholic persuasion, and their exemplary deportment, this society has obtained the patronage of the most distinguished individuals, and the kindly feelings of all who know the establishment.' Before moving to a new convent in Up Holland, Carmelite nuns occupied the Orrell Mount site from 1906 until 1917. In 1926 the clock at the gable end of the nunnery bell tower, which was made by Ainsworth of Warrington but which had been broken for about 25 years, was repaired by Mr. J. Highton of Pemberton.

16   In 1835 Orrell Mount, which was described as a 135 acre estate and consisted of land, houses, gardens, orchards and farm buildings, was advertised for sale by auction. At the rear of Orrell Mount, the sloping land, which was formerly a tip, had been terraced to create a 'delightful old world garden' where crocus flowers, trees and green grass created 'a charming effect' on sunny mornings. It was sometimes compared to Kew Gardens. Worrell's Directory of 1869 recorded that the gardens were 'now much resorted to'. Likewise, the Postal Directory of 1885 described the estate as 'of considerable extent, the grounds of which form at present a pleasure garden for the neighbourhood'. In July 1935 the terraced gardens were used for a garden party, organized by the owner, Abraham Guest, to raise funds for the Wigan and District Women's Free Church Council. Councillor Guest was active in the education sphere and the local comprehensive school was named after him.

Particulars

OF THE

ORRELL MOUNT ESTATE

AND PREMISES,

IN ORRELL, NEAR WIGAN,

In the County of Lancaster,

AND ALSO OF OTHER

HOUSES, LANDS, AND PREMISES,

Lying near thereto, and being in Orrell aforesaid,

AND CONTAINING IN THE WHOLE

135 Acres, 1 Rood, and 35 Perches of Land,

STATUTE MEASURE,

WHICH WILL BE SOLD BY AUCTION,

BY MESSRS. THOS. WINSTANLEY & SONS,

AT THE HOUSE OF

Mrs. Mawson, the Eagle and Child Inn, in Wigan,

IN THE COUNTY OF LANCASTER,

On WEDNESDAY, the 14th day of JULY, 1834,

At Four o'clock in the Afternoon.

The Mansion House, Shrubberies, and Pleasure Grounds, may be viewed on Monday, the 9th, and Wednesday, the 11th of June, or any subsequent Monday or Wednesday, between the hours of One and Five o'clock in the Afternoon, by Tickets, which, with Particulars and Lithographic Plans of the Premises and of the Mansion House, may may be obtained on application to Messrs. THOS. WINSTANLEY and SONS, Chorlton-street, Liverpool; Mr. ROBERT WINSTANLEY, Wigan; Winstanley, or at the Office of RALPH LEIGH, Attorney-at-Law, Wigan; where, or from Mr. DAGLISH, Civil Engineer, Orrell Cottage, any further information may be had.—The other parts of the Premises may be viewed on application to the Tenants.

17   At the southern end of the village the Grapes Inn was the central feature of the four 'Lane Ends' at Far Moor. This photograph shows the Grapes Inn in 1906. As the name on the board above the inn sign showed, the licence of the Grapes belonged to Mary Nixon, who succeeded her late husband and remained the tenant for Oldfield's brewery for nearly twenty years. The horse and cart in the background delivered paraffin and petrol; the lettering on the cart advertised White Rose American lamp oil and Pratt's Perfection Spirit, which was an early motor car fuel. (The Pratt Spirit Company had a storage depot in Pottery Lane in Wigan and petrol was distributed in tankers serving the local area.) The Grapes was the focal point of the Far Moor area. As part of the Silver Jubilee celebrations for King George V and Queen Mary in May 1935 about six hundred schoolchildren from the village schools assembled at the Grapes Inn, before walking in procession to Holgate playground for organized festivities.

18 Moor Road also formed part of the cross-roads at the Grapes Inn. At their bakery, next to Holgate School, at 171 Moor Road, the Haskayne family made bread, cakes and pies from 'As You Like It Flour' and they were the 'Best On The Market'. In winter children from the school used to warm their hands on the wall on which the ovens were located. Henry Haskayne distributed the confectionery to houses throughout the village by means of the cart drawn by his horse, Jim. On Mondays they went further afield to Ashton selling their home-made black puddings and brawn. They also supplied shops in Wigan and on Saturdays they sold as many as five hundred barm cakes filled with roast pork to Wigan rugby spectators as they left Central Park after matches. Orrell Post was similarly supplied with confectionery by the small bakery, which was established in 1904, adjacent to the Primitive Methodist Chapel.

19   Church Street was the centre of social, religious and commercial activity in Far Moor. Edward Hall, editor of Ellen Weeton's 'Diary of a Governess', described Far Moor in 1820 as a 'debased, vulgar, brutal district' populated by 'illiterate weavers and miners, just emerging from the barbarism of the eighteenth century and their slightly worse womenfolk'. According to a local newspaper in 1875, Far Moor remained 'an outlandish place … where the only signs of civilization are several public houses and a paltry railway station'. The ribbon development along the road was characterized by little houses built of 'grimy stone'. Despite the poverty, the inhabitants of Far Moor were very loyal and used every royal event to make the streets more colourful. The 'city of little hommers' celebrated the Golden Jubilee of Queen Victoria in 1887 with a display of flags and buntings and all 'mak o'things' such as coloured paper and calico, window and bed valances, and table covers.

20 Social life in Church Street was centred on the churches and public houses. In 1922 about 150 attended the Old Folks' treat, which included a meal at the Methodist Church, a concert in the Congregational Church, a packet of tea for the women and tobacco for the men. There was a great variety of social life; in 1910 one man 'got his leg broken with wrestling' in the Rose and Crown. There were also foot races for money and competitive rat killing; Jimmy Shaw's dog, Jacko, could kill 1,000 rats in less than 100 minutes! Most people had nick-names; Johnny Flannell,

Billy Poncake, and Johnny Dog were just a few of the characters. The commercial importance of Church Street was indicated by a 1903 directory that listed the following tradesmen:

butchers, nail makers, stone mason, drapers, inn keepers, iron monger, house furnisher, clog and shoe maker, painter and decorator, watch and clock maker, and grocers.

Cadman Brothers were nail makers, coal merchants and wagonette proprietors.

21 In the early 20th century, the policy of Williams Deacon's Bank was 'one of steady expansion wherever reasonable prospects of satisfactory business and deposits showed themselves'. Thus the board authorized Orrell's first bank by 'the purchase of premises … for £250 suitable for a new sub-branch' at 6 Church Street. It commenced trading on 7 March 1922 and by the end of the year the new branch had 52 accounts and acted as treasurer to the Orrell Urban District Council. The continued economic expansion of Orrell was reflected in the growth of the branch; structural alterations were made to the property during 1929 and 1930 and the number of accounts rose from 220 in 1929 to 297 in 1939. Now named The Royal Bank of Scotland, it continues to provide a high quality service to the local community. For a history of the bank see the newsletter of the Wigan Heritage Service, 'Past Forward' Spring 1998. The photograph is reproduced by kind permission of The Royal Bank of Scotland plc.

22 The ancient craft of bolt, screw and nail making was described in 'A Village of Smiths' by S. S. Swithaine, published in Wide World Magazine in 1907. Far Moor was one of the 'quaint little hamlets in Lancashire' where the nail making industry persisted 'almost exactly as it was hundred of years ago'. Nailsmiths gathered together 'clannishly' in villages like Far Moor, where there was once as many as fifty family smithies. Historically, Far Moor was characterized by 'narrow streets and alleys that twist and curve about tortuously'. Dicconson's foundry in Church Street was the centre of the industry. The sights and sounds remained constant for centuries. 'The hammers ring and clang incessantly. … The bellows blow, the sparks fly, and the heated irons are beaten into many shapes, while the nailers sweat over fire and anvil in their quaint old stone built smithies … and all the country round echoes to their anvil strokes.'

23 Nail making was a very conservative industry. Many of the skilled craftsmen worked in the same smithies all their lives and used the same equipment and methods as their predecessors. The basic raw material was brought into the smithies as bundles of iron rods of varying weight, length and thickness. Several rods of iron were put into the furnace. With his left hand the craftsman blew the bellows and with his right hand trimmed the furnace and handled the reddening irons. Once the required heat had been reached, the smith took a rod out of the fire and hammered it on his small 'stithy' to the shape desired. Every nail was made on the end of an iron rod and then cut off. As the smith beat the iron, he worked with his foot a small blowpipe, which fanned the heated end of the bar that was being beaten into an even greater glow. In 1865 they tried to form a trade union to alleviate the 'unfair system' that placed them under 'the most shameful bondage and tyrannical despotism'.

24 The nailers produced nails, bolts, screws, hinges, locks and many other items for use in 'the building of almost every structure' including ships, houses and carriages. Many different nails were made in the smithies and each had its distinctive features and name, such as diamonds, roseheads, horseshoes, shingles and sparrowbills. The sparrowbill (so called because it resembled a sparrow's beak) was a small nail used by shoemakers in the sole of the stronger kinds of boots and shoes, especially in the heel. It had no head, being driven into the leather until the top was level with the surface of the sole. There was a great demand for this particular nail; thousands of tons were used by shoemakers every year. A skilled nailsmith could supply sparrowbills at the incredible speed of five per minute or over 3,000 every working day. Before the coming of the railway, the nails, bolts, screws, hinges, locks and other items were transported from the village in horse-drawn carts.

25 William Dickinson was still making 1,200 nails a day at 77 years of age. In 1865, when the nailmakers were campaigning for a trade union, skilled workmen could earn 20 shillings a week, but most received 15 shillings and 'poor workmen' were paid only 5 shillings, despite working 15 hours a day, out of which they had to 'find their own fire and steel'. In fact, the workmen rarely saw any money since the 'truck system' operated. The master nailer owned the 'Tommy shop' where the workmen had to go to buy 'the necessaries of life of the poorest kind at the most exorbitant prices'. Sugar was 7d a pound and 'as brown as a brick' whilst a loaf cost 13d and was 'flat as a fluke'. By the early 20th century, the wages of a smith had fallen to 'half a crown for his day's work' and he needed to be 'a fleet man at his work to get that'. A man could start work at eight o'clock in the morning and work hard for twelve hours and still 'not have a pound clear for himself in a whole week'.

26 The nail making industry provided work for all the family. The heavy work required hardy men with 'a trained and practised eye and a strong and precise arm'. In the making of large nails and bolts, the smith used very heavy hammers worked by the foot by means of a treadle and it was 'all foot and hard work'. Children as young as 6 years of age blew the bellows and sorted the nails and bolts. Women undertook lighter tasks such as finishing the bolts. After the iron left the anvil and was cooled down, women put the spiral screw on the end that was turned into the 'nut' using a machine called a 'die'. The girl could put the screw end on 17 or 18 gross of bolts each day, so that about 2,500 bolts passed through her hands in a day. In their 1865 campaign for better working and living conditions the families invited inspection of their cottages, which were 'clean but destitute of those comforts' that were 'found in the dwellings of other working men's homes'.

27 Orrell was also noted for the excellent quality of its coal, 'the getting of which employs many of the labouring population' in local pits. In the 1840s Reverend Joshua Paley of St. John's Church observed that 'there were very few families in which one or more deaths have not occurred from accidents in the pits, in many, three or four have died thus. Few weeks pass in which some awful occurrence does not take place'. In 1857 an 8-year-old boy was crushed to death by wagons at Walthew House Colliery. In May 1872, at the same colliery, a boiler exploded with 'a terrific report'. For-tunately it was 'pay Monday' and the escape of the few miners who were in work was described as 'something marvellous'. In November 1932 the chimney of Walthew House Colliery, which had 'leaned acutely in the direction of Southport', was blown over in a gale. The structure was 140 feet high and its 30,000 bricks weighed hundreds of tons and when it collapsed it demolished the old pit engine house.

28 Donald Anderson in his book 'The Orrell Coal-field 1700-1850' commented on the engineering skill of Robert Daglish, who managed the Orrell Collieries. By 1813 Daglish had built a railway to serve the collieries and constructed a steam powered locomotive called the 'Yorkshire Horse' to run on it. Until comparatively recently, coal mines and other works continued to be served by steam trains. One engine transported coal from the rail sidings at Orrell to fire the kilns at Bispham Hall Brick and Terra Cotta Company. In July 1929 Mr. W. Moyers, Managing Director of Bispham Hall, officially opened the new recreation clubhouse and bowling green in Smethurst Road. The social club, which contained two billiard tables and several card tables, was built by the 200 workmen employed by the company. Orrell had a number of other brick-works, including Orrell Brick and Tile Company where, in January 1933, for the first time in the history of brick making in Wigan plastic bricks were made.

29   For many years Sandbrook cotton spinning mill, located by the Liverpool to Wigan railway line, was the only large manufacturing industry in Orrell. Built in the 1860s, Worrall's directories of 1869 and 1872 referred to the Widdows family as the proprietors; R. H. Widdows, 'cotton spinner', was amongst the first twelve members of the Orrell Local Board in 1872. It was a well run and respected company and it was a shock when it was summoned in 1907 for 'time cribbing'. On a visit to the mill on 7 May 1907, Government Inspectors of Factories and Workshops discovered machinery that should have been switched off at 5.30 p.m. was still running 'fully four minutes beyond that time' and the names were taken of thirty persons who were still working when the mill should have been stopped. The Company pleaded guilty and explained that the engineer had been called away by the foreman and had overlooked the time. It was the Company's first summons and they were fined £32.

30 In 1913 Signal Spinning Company Limited erected a new factory close to their Sandbrook Mill. The architects were Messrs. Unwin and Holland of Wigan and the builders were Messrs. Massey Brothers of Pemberton. Built at a cost of £30,000, it employed 150 to 200 people. On 30 May 1914 a social gathering took place to celebrate the completion of the new Signal Mill. Mr. F. Horne, the respected manager of both mills, invited the workforce to a tea and social. About 200 enjoyed the 'excellent repast' provided by the Parisian Bread Company of Wigan. Music was provided by Mr. Cuerden's band. At the interval Mr. Jos Pilkington, on behalf of the workforce, presented Mr. Horne with a handsome oak roll top desk. In addition to its economic importance, Sandbrook Spinning Company made significant contributions to the community. When the Young Men's Christian Association (YMCA) appealed for funds to establish a clubhouse in Orrell in 1919 the manager of the Mill contributed £100.

31   Generations of Orrell women and children were employed at Sandbrook Mill. Pupils were allowed to leave school if they attained the 'required standard' in tests and had perfect attendance; one mother went to St. Luke's Girls' School 'to request the lending of the attendance registers so as to prove that her daughter was able to work full time'. Other children worked part time at the factory whilst still at school. The Inspector of 'half timers' in mills was responsible for their continued progress and attendance at school. Thus in October 1879 the Inspector visited St. Luke's Girls' School to determine whether the pupils working at Orrell Cotton Mill 'attended regularly'. The system was not always successful. One Inspector recorded that 'the half timers with one or two exceptions are very backward'. Another regretted that girls of only 10 years of age were allowed to leave school because in Orrell they are 'running wild until they are 13 as half timers are rarely employed'.

32 Orrell station was opened in 1848 and until well into the 20th century it continued to be one of the most important stations in the district, serving a large population and with a 'remarkable' number of passengers using it daily. In 1881 the Orrell Local Board were concerned at the dangers to passengers having to cross the line at the station because 'the fast trains came upon them in a moment'. Requests by Orrell Urban District Council in 1895 to have entrances and booking offices on both sides of the line were rejected by the Lancashire and Yorkshire Railway Company. In 1910 vigilant station staff dealt with a major incident when a goods train from Liverpool emerged from the Up Holland tunnel with one of its trucks loaded with raw cotton on fire. Station staff detached the stricken wagon and extinguished the fire, but not before considerable damage had been done to the wagons and to 40 or 50 bales of raw cotton destined for East Lancashire mills.

33   For those who could afford the licence fee, the horse and trap offered a sedate means of travel. For other people all sorts of carriers operated a local transport system. According to Worrall's Directory of 1872 horse-drawn 'omnibuses' passed through Orrell several times daily. In 1874 George William Nickson and John Hughes were summoned before Wigan Magistrates for racing their vehicles. Passengers complained that Hughes drove an omnibus at such a furious speed that one of the horses was 'pulled off its legs'. He refused to slow down and the passengers were 'placed in great danger'. The situation was made worse by the rutted roads. Prior to 1872 Orrell had a Highway Board, which levied a rate to be spent on the maintenance of roads. The ratepayers met in the National School at Far Moor to appoint a Surveyor of Highways, whose task it was to ensure that the work was completed. Clearly, improved roads and better public transport were necessary for the growing village.

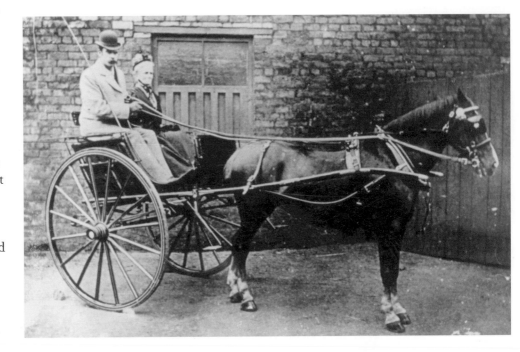

34 From the 1880s Wigan Corporation rendered services as Transport Authority to Orrell. In the early 1880s the Wigan Tramway Company sought permission from Orrell Local Board to extend the tramway to Orrell and to replace horse-drawn vehicles with steam-powered trams. In 1898 the Tramway Company was supported by a 'memorial signed by 623 inhabitants of the Townships' of Orrell and Up Holland requesting improved services. In 1906 Orrell Urban District Council agreed to the electrification of the route to Abbey Lakes, on condition that lighting, widening and other necessary works were completed by Wigan Corporation and that 'cars should not exceed 12 miles an hour in Orrell Road'. It was not always a comfortable arrangement and over the next 26 years there were difficulties in providing tram transport to the Orrell area. There were frequent complaints about overcrowding, high fares, poor track condition and lack of shelters at the Orrell Post stop and the Abbey Lakes terminus.

ORRELL RD.ORRELL

35 Snow at Orrell Post presented particular problems to the tram company and to the local councils. In 1911 Orrell Urban District Council offered to relieve Wigan Corporation of their obligation to remove snow from the Orrell Road, after it had been cleared from the tram track by the Corporation. Orrell Council offered to undertake this responsibility in exchange for an annual sum equivalent to a rate of £2 per furlong. Alternatively, Orrell Council was prepared to clear and remove the snow from the tram track if Wigan Corporation agreed to pay the actual costs incurred. Wigan Council preferred the first suggestion but was only willing to pay 30 shillings per furlong. By the 1930s the policy of Wigan Corporation was to replace the loss making trams by trackless petrol omnibuses, operating a municipal service between Wigan and parts of Orrell. The last tram to Abbey Lakes ran on Saturday 28 March 1931, with a through bus service coming into operation on the following day.

36   In June 1919 Wigan Corporation used a motor bus in its experimental transport service, linking Billinge to the Wigan Corporation electric tramway at Orrell Post. The picture showed the first bus on Saturday 25 October 1919 outside the Stag Inn, which served as the meeting point of the two systems. The service opened up new horizons for local people. One man from Billinge declared: 'I've never been to Orrell Post for 30 years or more.' Many others took advantage of the new link to experience the shopping facilities and social attractions of Wigan. During the 1930s Mark Cadman of Orrell applied to Wigan Corporation for licences to operate an omnibus service between Wigan and Orrell, claiming that the service operated by the Ribble Bus Company was inadequate for the district. Many Orrell people preferred to use Cadman's service because that company offered 'contract tickets' which enabled Orrell residents, employed in Wigan, to go home for a midday meal.

he first motor-bus of the Wigan Corporation
[running between Orrell & Billinge in 1919. Outside the]
[Stag] Inn at Orrell Post.

37   Off Church Street, in areas like the 'Square' and the 'Glasshouses', many families lived in small cottages with inadequate water supply and sewerage systems. An Orrell Local Board survey in 1873 revealed the extent of the problems. Supplies of water were obtained from ponds, streams, old pit shafts, ditches and wells. Sally's Well, the only reliable source of water at Far Moor, was liable to serious contamination. Some people carried water from a source near Gathurst station, 'a distance altogether unreasonable'. Alternatively, occupants purchased water of 'doubtful purity' in cans from water carts at a cost of 6d to 8d per week. In one case twenty houses were served by only two privies, which were of an 'unfit and filthy description'. Other 'great nuisances' included 'masses of putrid filth' associated with 'overflowing cesspools and privies and an open ditch full of stagnant offensive matter'.

38 Dr. G.W. Johnstone was appointed as Orrell's first Medical Officer of Health in 1874. In his reports to the Local Board he highlighted the diseases afflicting Orrell and linked them to the age and state of the dwellings, and the concomitant problems of overcrowding. In Church Street itself many large families lived in neat but small terraced houses. However, in the squares off Church Street many families existed in one-bedroom cottages. These problems were compounded by the keeping of pigs and poultry on the premises. Living conditions were made worse by the unpaved and unclean condition of yards into which all sorts of obnoxious deposits, slops and other liquid filth were thrown. The Medical Officer also complained about the habits of the people, including the 'very offensive smell' caused by 'cooking chipped potatoes in oil'. Improvements to the housing stock had to await slum clearance schemes and new housing estate developments initiated by Orrell Urban District Council.

39 With such appalling living conditions it was inevitable that diseases such as smallpox, scarlatina, scarlet fever, whopping cough, measles and typhus were rife in Orrell. One cause of the spread of such diseases was the 'thoughtless inter communication' on the part of the people with infections and the practice of 'allowing children to run about the streets imperfectly cured'. In 1907 Orrell Urban District Council debated the establishment of a small hospital in which infected patients could be isolated: 'In case of an outbreak of smallpox they had hardly any provision at all.' In 1914 the Wigan and District Smallpox Hospital Committee considered a number of sites. A field on the west side of Jackson's Lane (Gathurst Road), overlooking Dean Wood, seemed to offer the ideal, remote location. In the end, Orrell Council opted not to build its own isolation hospital. It was often left to churches in Orrell to alleviate suffering, poverty and ignorance.

40 On 1 December 1699, Reverend Thomas Young leased five acres of land in Spring Road and established a Mission at Crossbrook where Roman Catholics in Orrell could worship in secrecy and avoid religious persecution. The rent for the site was £11 per year and in spite of the poverty of many parishioners, gifts and donations were made to support the Mission. Towards the end of the 18th century religious toleration for Catholics was accepted officially. By the Catholic Relief Act of 1778 the celebration of mass became legal; in 1784 Bishop Matthew Gibson confirmed 54 people and there were 170 Easter communicants. A Second Catholic Relief Act in 1791 allowed Catholics to build and use licensed chapels and, in 1804, Reverend Thomas Kaye was sent to make a new beginning at Crossbrook. The original Crossbrook Mission 'was removed by the consent of the Bishop' and a new chapel was built on the site of Moor Ditch at Far Moor and given the name Serenus Place and later St. James' Church.

41 The new St. James' Church was enlarged in 1841 and by 1865 the congregation numbered 580 and fifty children attended the Catechism instruction every Sunday. The Church itself had no tower and no chancel and was 'not warmed'. There was a Sunday School 'but none at night'. However, a coeducational parish school had been established by 1848. The boys and girls were 'not entirely separated in school, but they were in the playground'. Religious instruction was given every day by the teachers and the priest visited the school 'almost daily'. The day school was supported by 'an annual charity sermon and the pennies of the scholars' and was extended in the 1870s. A tower and belfry were added to the church itself in 1870 and a new bell was consecrated to mark its centenary in 1904. In 1922 a side chapel was built in memory of ten parishioners who died in the First World War. In July 1927 a service was held to mark the opening of the Grotto to our Lady of Lourdes at St. James' Church.

42 A temporary Congregational Church was established at Far Moor in 1810 and by 1812 the Sunday School had 130 scholars. In 1820 Reverend John Holgate came to Orrell and was the Minister for thirty years. In her Journal, Ellen Weeton recorded how she left home in Up Holland to teach at the Sunday School 'setting out soon after eight, and dining in the Chapel on currant bun, as I had to teach all afternoon; and often staying evening service, so that I did not return home till at night. The girls were exceedingly attentive (and) increased in numbers'. The permanent Salem Church was built in 1824 and in 1825 special sermons were preached at the 'Dissenting Chapel' with collections taken to help towards 'liquidating the debt' on the new Church. As late as the 1930s, Orrell Congregational Church, 'just hidden behind the main thoroughfare' with its 'plain unpretentious fabric' was still known as 'Holgate's Chapel'. After his death in 1850 a plaque in his memory was erected in Salem Church.

SACRED
TO THE MEMORY OF
THE REV. JOHN HOLGATE
30 YEARS THE MINISTER OF THIS CHURCH
WHO DIED NOVEMBER 25TH. 1850
AGED 65 YEARS.
HE WAS A GOOD MAN A PIOUS CHRISTIAN
AND IN HIM HIS FLOCK LOST
A GOOD AND FAITHFUL SHEPHERD.

43 The success of the churches in Orrell was demonstrated in 1880 when over eight hundred scholars and friends from Orrell Congregational School, the Primitive Methodist School, Orrell Post School and Tontine Sunday School assembled at Salem Church to celebrate an Orrell Sunday School Centenary. Salem Church developed further during the successful pastorate of Reverend John Whitton (1883-1917) who, like John Holgate, was also an advocate of education. The Church was rebuilt in 1905 and this provided a valuable additional assembly facility for the community; in May 1906 a large congregation heard Brigadier Holmes give a lecture on the Salvation Army. In 1912 a new Sunday School was erected at the rear of Salem Church. It consisted of eight classrooms grouped round a main assembly hall; the classrooms were for young men and women and younger scholars and there was a primary department for 120 infants. The whole building could be transformed into one large hall for public meetings and concerts.

44 Reverend John Holgate was 'an earnest educationalist' and he established an elementary day school in Orrell. In Slater's Directory of 1848 it was described as an 'orphan school', with John Holgate as its master. However, the progress of Holgate School was limited by lack of resources and it closed in 1867. In 1875 Holgate School was opened again with Miss Jane Marsden as headmistress, a position she held until 1923. In 1882 arrangements were completed with the Board of Education for placing the Holgate School under government inspection. The academic progress of the pupils was retarded by the physical condition of the building, which was 'anything but what it should be' and the pupils were 'taught at great inconvenience in the old buildings'. There was a 'poor gallery' in which 'the seats have no back rests' and there were very few suitable desks. Government inspectors ordered the managers to provide better accommodation and facilities 'with as little delay as possible'.

45   During the incumbency of Reverend John Whitton at Salem Church from 1883 to 1917, the foundation stone of the new portion of Holgate School was laid in 1892 by Mr. Crossfield of Liverpool, at whose request the name of John Holgate was inscribed on the stone. The enlarged school opened on 4 April 1893 and, in addition to classes, it hosted social events such as the annual concert of the Holgate Cricket Club. When the new Salem Sunday School was completed, Holgate became an elementary day school under the control of Lancashire County Council. On the eve of the First World War it was reorganized as an infants' school; 32 pupils transferred from Holgate to upper schools in 1919. A further reorganization took place in 1923 when Holgate became a Senior Mixed School with Mr. F. Davies as headmaster. When the school reopened on 3 September 1923 most of the 123 children in attendance came from 'two neighbouring schools' and a small number from 'a more distant Council School'.

Rev. JOHN WHITTON.

46   In 1928 no new pupils were admitted to Holgate School 'owing to the reorganization pending' and all the children were transferred to St. James' Road Council School. It was re-opened as a Junior and Infant School under the headship of Mr. Joseph Calderbank with 150 boys and girls, aged 4 years and upwards, being taught in five classes. Education officials found the headmaster to be 'interested in his school' and anxious to improve the academic performance of the school and to widen the curriculum. The managers were 'pleased to find a marked improvement in the chil-dren generally'. During the 1930s successful innovations included field work excursions, special events such as an Animal Week in 1934, and the purchase of Mr. Holt's field behind the school for use as a playing field. Government Inspectors confirmed that Holgate had become 'a well conducted school'. The headmaster and his staff were 'commended for the de-lightful atmosphere of joyous activity' that permeated the school.

47   In October 1935 Holgate House, for so long associated with Reverend John Holgate, was demolished. The house, which dated back to 1710, was built in stone with a gable end wall a yard thick. In 1822 the parlour was the venue for an awkward meeting involving Mr. Holgate and 'a set of people consisting entirely of colliers, weavers, and labourers' who were to consider Miss Ellen Weeton's application to join the Church. Despite her rejection, Miss Weeton believed John Holgate to be 'a most worthy man'. In 1928 Orrell Urban District Council considered a proposal to change the name of the road that linked Far Moor with Orrell Post from Moor Road to Holgate Road in honour of Reverend Holgate. The Council rejected the proposition on the grounds that John Holgate's name had been perpetuated by the school that bore his name in Moor Road. Some of the stone from the demolished Holgate House was used in the creation of a sunken garden in Marl Grove on the new housing estate off Sandy Lane.

48 During the latter years of the 19th century Mr. and Mrs. J.H. Aldred made Holgate House a major social centre in Orrell. Mrs. Aldred presided over the weekly meetings of the Holgate Literary and Social Circle. In November 1894 Mrs. Aldred, from the Chair, outlined the object of the society and, after referring to the various institutions which existed in Orrell with links to John Holgate, trusted that this one would exceed all its predecessors in terms of numbers and good results. The activities of the Circle included musical evenings, games and meals. The Society also had a programme of lectures; in February 1895 Miss Whitton gave a talk on 'The position of women in the past, present and future'. In 1889 Mrs. Aldred presented Henry Atherton, aged 11 of Church Street, with the Royal Humane Society award for his bravery in rescuing a 6-year-old boy who, on his way home from Holgate School, had accidentally fallen to the bottom of the 40 yards deep shaft of the disused Burgy Pit.

49   Independent Methodism at Lamberhead Green dates from the 1830s and during the 1840s members 'engaged a large room and commenced a Sunday School'. In 1848 the 'new chapel' was in 'a fair way for prosperity'. In the 1850s this 'little Free Gospel Church' was well attended, not least when their temperance crusade proved to be the 'first step to the house of God to several poor drunkards'. By 1860 the congregation was 'on the decrease owing principally to the uncomfortableness of the place' and a new school cum chapel building was erected in Fleet Street 'to make the congregation more comfortable'. During the 1860s few members escaped the 'evil effects' and poverty caused by the Cotton Famine but they were 'beginning to clear the debt off our little Chapel'. Successful missionary work in the district ensured that the Chapel was 'literally crammed' and they opened a 'preaching place' in nearby Kitt Green where 'much wickedness has existed, but we believe good has been effected'.

NEW CHAPEL, LAMBERHEAD GREEN.

50 During the 1870s Lamberhead Green Independent Methodist Chapel finally cleared its debts and, whereas in the past it had been 'scarcely recognized by some of the neighbouring Churches', it now 'obtained and maintained a position equal with any'. In 1887 a new chapel, Gothic in design, was erected on land to the rear, facing Loch Street, with seating for 270. The new chapel was opened for worship on 19 February 1888. The opening services in the new chapel were attended by large congregations of people of every denomination and a great number who belonged to no place of worship. At the same time more Sunday School accommodation was urgently needed, but it was not until 5 August 1895 that the foundation stones were laid for new Sunday School premises to replace the old rooms, which were pulled down. The school, which cost about £1,200, was officially opened in December 1895, money being raised by concerts, teas, entertainment and sales of work.

51   In the early 1840s about 18 members of the Methodist Society held services and a Sunday School in Crab Tree Lane or Church Street. By 1846 the members felt 'at liberty to build a Chapel if providence favoured them with the means', but it was only on 16 October 1859 that the chapel was opened, the result of 'a very worthy effort made by very poor working class people'. On 6 April 1870 the Trustees decided 'That as soon as the Members of the Sunday School had raised £50 a Committee would be formed to consider the building of a new School'. The new school, consisting of a main hall and a classroom at the rear of the chapel, was opened in December 1875. In June 1907 a service of thanksgiving was held to celebrate the clearance of the building debts. However, in the early hours of 9 February 1910, a fire gutted the church and Sunday School. It took four hours to get the fire under control; the school premises were completely destroyed and only the shell of the chapel remained.

52 The members and trustees of Orrell Methodist Church took immediate action after the devastating fire. On 11 February 1910 they accepted an offer from the insurance company of £450 to cover the loss of the chapel and Sunday School. Local builders, Messrs. Clough and Gaskell, were commissioned to build the new school church which was designed by Mr. Smithson, an architect from Leeds. The foundation stone was laid on 14 July 1910 and Far Moor was decorated with streamers, buntings and banners to celebrate the event. The new 'Centenary Memorial School' was officially opened on 5 November 1910 and it was anticipated that the building of the new school would be followed by the erection of a new church. By the 1930s, when Reverend W.R. Reid was the Minister, the accommodation was considered inadequate for the 253 members, 345 Sunday School scholars, 222 senior and junior members of the Christian Endeavour, 45 teachers and officials. A new church with a modern design was opened in 1964.

PRIMITIVE METHODIST CHURCH,
ORRELL.

REV. W. R. REID.

53   In the 1850s, when Orrell Post consisted of 'but a few working men's cottages', class meetings and Sunday services were held in the open air and at a cottage occupied by Daniel Baldwin at 8 Moor Road with Thomas Winstanley as Class Leader. By 1860 the Mission had moved to the corner of Smith's Road (now Gathurst Road). Services and a Sunday School were held in the room, the entrance to which was effected by ascending an outside staircase and hence the meeting place was always referred to as 'Upsteps'. Eventually on 15 May 1875 the foundation stone of the present Orrell Post Primitive Methodist Chapel was laid by Mr. T. Rigby of Crawford Village and Mr. J. Anders of Holland Moor. The simple building cost about £600 and, in addition to its primary religious function, it became a centre of social life at Orrell Post. Thus three evening lectures in 1884 given by Reverend J. Prestwick of Bolton on his visit to America on a Cunard steamship were attended by very large congregations.

54 By 1911 it was necessary to provide better facilities at the old Orrell Post Chapel and plans were prepared for a new frontage with a gallery to hold sixty people and two classrooms underneath. Bazaars, tea parties and concerts were organized to raise money to clear £35 debt on the old chapel and to cover the £100 cost of the new extension, which was opened in September 1913. After the First World War, the chapel continued an active existence and by the 1930s a further extension of the church was deemed necessary to meet the demands of a growing population, especially in the Linden Avenue area. A Building Fund was launched by Reverend H.T. Wigley, who was well supported by members. This extension consisted of the schoolroom premises built on the side of the church and was officially opened in September 1932. The capacity of the new building was tested when visiting lecturers, such as Reverend H.J. Pickett, Principal of Hartley Victoria College, came to Orrell Post.

A GRAND
Christmas Bazaar
OF USEFUL AND FANCY ARTICLES

Will be held in connection with the

PRIMITIVE METHODIST CHURCH, ORRELL POST,

on the three following dates :—

Wednesday, December 12th, Thursday, December 13th, and

Saturday, (Children's Day,) December 15th, 1928.

55 Orrell's only Baptist Church was formed on Sunday 6 April 1851. Earlier a number of local people had left the Church of England, disillusioned by the 'preaching', and met first in a house and then in a rented room. By 1862 the hired room used was too 'small, close and badly ventilated' to accommodate the increased numbers of members. Hence, at a church meeting on 6 July 1864, the idea of building a chapel was discussed. The necessary land was given free by Jane Farrimond and Jireh Chapel was opened on Sunday 23 October 1864. Jane's brother, Henry, was a major figure in the early history of Jireh Chapel, where he became a deacon in 1860 and later a pastor and 'preached the gospel faithfully … for 16 years'. Jireh Chapel still serves the community in Orrell. For a history of Jireh Chapel see the newsletter of the Wigan Heritage Service, 'Past Forward' Spring 1999. The photograph is reproduced by kind permission of Pam Thomas and Christine Berry.

56 Reverend Joshua Paley of St. John's Anglican Church at Pemberton was concerned by the living conditions and habits of local people. 'The habits of these men, especially the colliers, are so bad that the utmost difficulties are thrown in our way of communicating instruction'. He believed that education was the way forward and in 1841 he leased a piece of land from John Ashurst of Far Moor to be 'applied as a site for poor people … and for no other purpose'. In 1843 a National School was built on the site; prior to that date girls had been instructed in a club room at the Rose and Crown public house, whilst boys were taught at Rivington Brook Inn. The demand was so great that the building proved inadequate to meet the requirements of the district until 1883 when two 'commodious' rooms were added, having been financed by local coal proprietors and by a series of festivities. The use of the school was restricted to girls and infants and a separate provision was sought for the boys.

57   For more than thirty years, a week night service was conducted in the school but on 11 July 1874 the foundation stone of the first Anglican Church in Orrell was laid. The building of the School Church of St. Luke was completed in the 1880s at a cost of £1,200. Up until then the facilities and resources were under pressure because the numbers of boys had 'increased considerably' but, according to a report by Government Inspectors in 1878, 'the same high standard of discipline and instruction' was being maintained. The new building had a dual function, serving as a school for boys and as a place of family worship. It was hoped that the new school would mean 'that the people of Far Moor would become more elevated in their tastes' and would link in with the drive to 'remove all the miserable shanties in the village'. The building hosted the Sunday School and the church services until 1912 when the children transferred to the new Council School that was built in St. James' Road.

58 The curriculum at the village schools was dominated by the 3Rs – reading, writing and arithmetic. Government Inspectors conducted annual tests in these key subjects. The tests were arranged in a series of standards and each child was expected to move up a standard each year. This testing of the three main subjects put teachers and pupils under stress and led to formal teaching, rote learning and severe disciplinary regimes. Being a Church of England school, religious instruction assumed a prominent place in the curriculum and the inspectors generally confirmed that it was 'very carefully given'. Elementary science, the geography and history of Britain and the British Empire were also taught alongside practical skills like sewing, hemming, seaming, stitching, buttonholing and darning. During the 1920s there were also lessons on the League of Nations Union. The academic work was broken up by physical training and drill and '10 minutes recreation' allowed in the morning.

59 In 1902 Reverend Forrest of St. John's Pemberton and Reverend Wills of St. Thomas' Up Holland requested the Bishop of Liverpool to agree to the formation of an Anglican missionary district at Orrell with its own Curate in charge. It was increasingly difficult for the clergy of the two neighbouring Anglican churches to service the growing population of Orrell and in 1903 Reverend M.C. Sydenham was appointed as the first Curate. Reverend Sydenham emphasized that he was licensed to the Bishop of Liverpool rather than to Up Holland or Pemberton vicars and he outlined the boundaries of his 'cure'. Church services in the old building had been far from ideal; those attending church services on Sunday had to sit at desks used by the boys during the week. Reverend P.C. Ingrouille set up a New Church Building Fund and under Reverend W.R. Johnson the New Church scheme began to make progress. Messrs. Austin and Paley produced the sketch plans for a new church.

PROPOSED   NEW   CHURCH   OF   ST.   LUKE   —   ORRELL

60   In 1915 Reverend A.D. Smart became Curate and later the first Vicar of the separate parish of St. Luke. Active fund raising was undertaken to support a new church on a site off Lodge Road offered by Mr. Bankes of Winstanley Hall. The new Church of St. Luke was eagerly anticipated by Reverend Smart. 'For many a long year the Church had been a dream, and many had become convinced that it always would be a dream, and nothing more. And now the Foundation Stone is to be laid. We shall be making history on that day.' The foundation stone was laid on 6 November 1926 and the consecration of the new church took place on 24 September 1927. In March 1932 the vicarage was completed and by 1937 £8,000 had been raised for the building of an extension of the church to the east, which comprised a chancel with choir and sanctuary, a Lady Chapel, vestries and organ chamber. It was built in a modified Gothic style with materials specially chosen to harmonize with the existing structure.

ST LUKES ORRELL 1926

61 The social life of many villagers was provided by the plethora of public houses in Orrell, which included the Stag, Red Lion, Colliers Arms, Fishergate Inn, Leigh Arms, Running Horses, Grapes, Queen's Arms, Rose and Crown and the Railway Inn. There was a history of disorderly beer houses in Orrell. In August 1855, Henry Nickson, whose beer house was 'one of the worst', was 'charged in the keeping his house open later than the time allowed by the law'. The public houses and beer shops were open for most of the day and whole families were very often 'found together in these places of iniquity'. The Orrell Local Board received numerous complaints about periodical disturbances, brutal outrages, Sabbath breaking, Sunday gambling, indecent conduct, rowdyism, fighting and 'disgraceful riots'. The problem was attributed to miners indulging in excessive drinking at beer shops and public houses; as its name implied, the Colliers Arms was the favourite haunt of many miners.

62   In May 1873 the Local Board sent a petition to Lieutenant Colonel Bruce, Head of Lancashire Police Constabulary, asking for an extra police officer to be stationed at Orrell Post to assist Sergeant John Bennett. In 1897 Orrell Urban District Council supported police moves to effect more control by forcing publicans to take out licences if music and singing occurred on the premises. The intention was to restrict such licences to appropriate pubs and to discourage young people from dancing 'from which very often demoralising and indecent behaviour takes place'. In 1922 the police were called in to investigate human remains unearthed during the restoration of the Stag Inn; foul play was suspected at first but it was later determined that a medical student had disposed of his skeleton in a shallow grave behind the pub! Over the years a number of public houses have been demolished or converted to other uses; the Black Horse Inn in Church Street became residential accommodation.

63 The Rose and Crown Inn, like most of Orrell's public houses, provided important functions for the community. The meetings of various lodges and sick and burial clubs were held in pubs; the Travellers' Rest hosted a Children's Burial Society with over 100 members and the Orrell Post Burial Society met at the Stag. Inquests into accidents and deaths were often held in public houses. The Rose and Crown was the headquarters of the Orrell Bowling Club. The Botanical Society met at the Fishergate Inn. Many pubs had angling clubs and fishing was the source of a conflict between Wigan Corpora-tion and Orrell Urban District Council after the First World War. During the 1920s fishermen from Wigan were allowed access to Orrell waterworks, the tender for which had been 'got by Hickman and Dovenor of Liverpool in 1876'. The intervention of Orrell Council could not persuade Wigan Corporation to allow Orrell fishermen to use the reservoirs on the same terms as those granted to Wigan anglers.

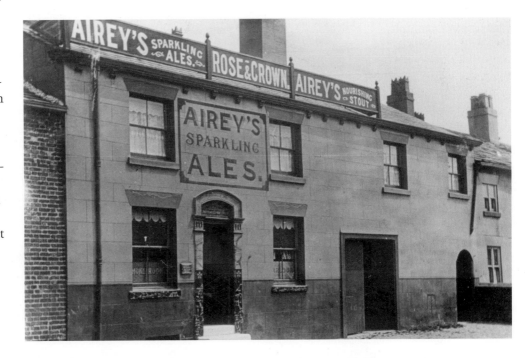

64 Traditional village social life was characterized by parties, walking days, sports and carnivals. In this picture girls from the village dressed up in carnival gear to tour the streets on the horse-drawn, decorated cart. It is sad that many village traditions have died out. One old custom was the Orrell Post plum fair, which was observed on the first moonlit Sunday night in September. Couples dressed themselves in fancy costumes to vie for the prize, which was always a basket of plums. The judge was usually one of the village elders, dressed up in female clothes, complete with bonnet and veil. Another man carried a lighted candle while the costumed judge looked down a 'tun dish' at the competing couples. By the early 20th century the plum fair had moved to the Old Engine Inn from its historical base in an old house nearby. Another village custom was the distribution of 'dow' or dole, which was paid in kind to the poor and included bread, calico, flannel and woollen cloth.

65 The various churches battled hard against the evils of excessive alcohol. On the 43rd Anniversary of the Independent Order of Rechabites in 1885, a speaker recalled how the streets of Orrell were once 'crowded with tea total processions'. Another delegate reiterated their aims of 'securing the young men from the public house society, and also reclaiming the drunkard'. A visiting speaker to the Orrell Congregational Band of Hope monthly meeting in 1896 gave numerous illustrations of 'the ruinous effects of intemperance' and entreated all the many present 'to pledge themselves not to taste the bane of our country'. Women attending the 1st Anniversary meeting of the Orrell Branch of the British Women's Temperance Association in 1887 were urged 'to rescue their sisters' who were 'the victims of strong drink' and were reminded of the benefits that accrued from total abstinence. In support of their aims, the various groups often held public meetings and services in the open air.

66   Orrell's churches offered an impressive range of facilities and attractions to counter the appeal of the public houses. The Sunday Schools provided the first universal system of basic religious, moral and secular education. Scholars, young and old, were introduced to the Bible, magazines, periodicals, catechisms and handbooks published specifically for use in the Sunday Schools. The churches were crucial to the inculcation of orderliness, punctuality, sobriety and other virtues, governing personal behaviour and social discipline. They were also major social and recreation centres offering outings, treats, processions, anniversary festivals, mutual improvement societies, music, classes, libraries, reading rooms, charity sermons, sick and burial clubs, cricket and football teams, galas, rallies and synods. Such attractions were important to the success of the different denominations in obtaining and maintaining converts and followers.

67 Like many churches, Orrell Primitive Methodists Chapel started a football team to encourage church attendance and affiliation. Not everybody supported the trend. In the Wigan Observer an 'anti footballer' asked: 'Does not football grow more attractive than religious worship and the rules of the game form a more interesting study than the rules of the Holy Writ?' He believed that football dragged participants into 'evil associations' and 'every form of vice' thus 'polluting the morality and contaminating with its iniquity the souls of hundreds of promising youths'. He expressed his antagonism in verse:

Football is a pleasure of a very
    rowdy kind
And is suitable only for the
    roughest of mankind,
It may be pleasing to the self
    imagined brave,
As it is to the betting, reckless,
    skipjack knave;

But men of culture, wisdom,
    sobriety, and reason
Will wisely unite to kick it out of
    season
And the speedy banishment of this
    wily foe
Will save young men from present
    folly and future woe.

ORRELL PRIMITIVES 1915

68 The 'reading room' off Church Street was a men's 'club' where occasional lectures were given and where members could play snooker and billiards. Other sporting activities in Orrell included wrestling, whippet racing, pigeon flying, rabbit coursing, starling shooting, 'piggy', pitch and toss, bowling and angling. However, the lack of playfields for young people was regretted by Reverend Whitton of Salem Church. He found it distressing to see children running about the streets and making a nuisance in Holgate schoolyard. Orrell Urban District Council eventually reacted by establishing playing fields at Bell Lane, Moor Road and Park Road. In 1933 the Council purchased the following facilities for Holgate playground: sandpits, a joy wheel, swings with cradle seats, swings with plain seats, a rocking horse and six seats. As part of the preservation of rural England campaign, Orrell Council took action to preserve Dean Wood and Redwood, 'a pretty dingle' that would make 'a nice retreat'.

69   In 1919 Wigan participated in the Red Triangle Campaign to continue the work, which the Young Men's Christian Association (YMCA) had performed during the First World War. The inauguration of a Red Triangle Club at Orrell helped to meet a growing demand in the neighbourhood for social intercourse, for fellowship and for moral, intellectual and physical guidance. There was a great deal of enthusiasm for the YMCA movement in Orrell and a good response to the appeal for help in establishing a permanent club building. Squire G.H. Bankes of Winstanley Hall provided two acres of land not far from Orrell station, Bispham Hall Colliery donated building materials and Signal Mill made a generous donation to the building fund, which was also boosted by the weekly contributions from employees of three local firms. The foundation stone was laid on 20 March 1920 by Sir A.K. Yapp, National YMCA Secretary, and the YMCA was opened on 28 October 1920 by Her Royal Highness Princess Marie Louise.

From a sketch by Miss R. V. Warters.

70 The Entertainment Committee of the YMCA arranged varied programmes of activities, including social evenings, whist drives, dances, concerts, study circles, meetings, lectures, boy scouts and girl guides. In April 1923 the Annual General Meeting of the Orrell branch of the League of Nations Union was held in the small hall. In May 1926 Liverpool physician Dr. J.C. Macalister delivered a lecture at the YMCA clubhouse in which he advocated sport as an ideal outlet for the superfluous energy of young people. In addition to the billiard and snooker room, outdoor facilities at the YMCA included a bowling green and a playing field. A very successful Football Club had been established and the young men of Orrell Red Triangle soccer team were crowned as champions of the Wigan Juvenile Organization Committee Welfare League in the season 1925 to 1926. They won 31 of their 34 games, scoring 119 goals and conceding only 27 goals. The YMCA also became the venue for rugby union games.

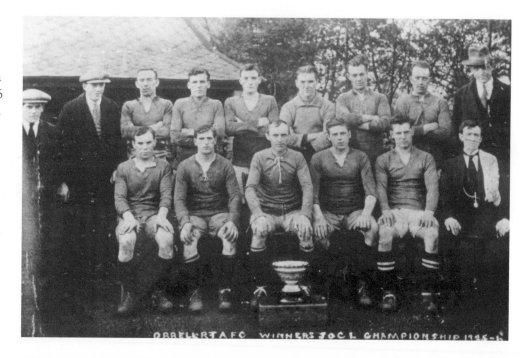

71   Orrell has become synonymous with rugby union. Orrell Rugby Union Football Club originated in 1927 with Squire G H Bankes as President and J C Simpkin as Chairman and Secretary. J W Liptrot captained the team in matches against local clubs. During the 1930s the club had a nomadic existence, using pitches at Walthew House Farm, Lamberhead Green Council School, Abbey Lakes, Orrell Mount, Alma Hill in Up Holland and on the Donkey Field in Billinge. The Stag Inn was often used for committee meetings and social events. In 1937 the club obtained a more permanent venue when a ground and hut were leased from the YMCA in Winstanley Road. The Second World War curtailed the supply of players and in 1940 it was 'resolved with deep regret that the Club should be suspended for the duration of the war'. The Club was reformed on 1 October 1945 and, particularly after the move to the Edge Hall Road site in 1950, Orrell Rugby Union Football Club went from strength to strength.

1930 · 31

BACK ROW: E.O. Bradley, F. Gaskell, W. Whitton, J.C. Millar, W. Calderbank, T. Derbyshire, R. Banks
R. Bushell, J.C. Simpkin, W.G. Ashcroft, R. Hartley, E. Hitchen, W. Parkinson, E. Unsworth.
MIDDLE ROW: D. Hartley, J. Anderton, J.W. Liptrot, W. Millar, E. Alker, W. Howarth.
FRONT ROW: J. Hickey, J. Lyon, J. Unsworth, R. Chadwick, J. Dougary.

72 During strikes like that of 1912, miners' families endured extreme hardship. Thousands of men, women and children picked coal from the slag heaps of Norley Hall Colliery, using picks and shovels and taking the coal to their homes in bags, buckets and wheelbarrows. The Lamberhead Green Relief Committee was set up to alleviate the suffering of the most needy families and especially children. In April 875 loaves of bread and 1,750 scones were distributed and the Committee prepared 10,000 meals consisting of potato hash, pea soup, bread, bacon, scones, buns and tea.

Likewise, during the Great Strike of 1926, the miners received assistance. Funds were provided to set up a clog shop at Orrell Post where the unemployed miners were taught to make and repair clogs for their children; their work had to be voluntary and no wages were paid to the men. The soup kitchen at Orrell YMCA, shown in this picture, fed two hundred children for twenty weeks on potato hash, pea soup, and meat and potato pies.

73 Abbey Lakes was 'the rendezvous of picnic parties and excursions from the larger towns in the neighbourhood, such a lake being attractive on account of the scarcity of water in the district'. The Orrell Local Board was concerned about the 'intolerable nuisances' associated with the 'public house and buildings' in the vicinity of 'the old mill dam'. The nuisances became intolerable at peak periods such as on Good Friday 1879: 'The yells and discordant notes from rival omnibus drivers, guards and other roughs was something fearful and the road was next to impassable for fully two hours.' Likewise, on 12 July each year thousands of spectators lined Orrell Road to witness members of the Orange Lodges make their annual pilgrimage to Abbey Lakes, which, by long custom, was something of a holiday Mecca for the 'Orangemen'. In 1928 it was estimated that 10,000 Orangemen descended on Abbey Lakes to enjoy the lake, the zoo, the scores of bands and 'numerous attractive tableaux'.

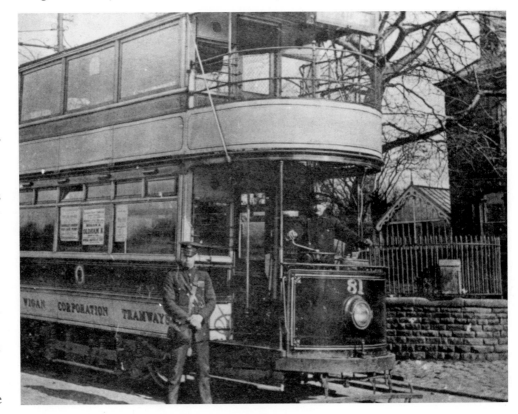

74 Dean Wood was one of the many local holiday haunts around 'smoky Wigan' that Harry Parkes photographed for local newspapers. Dean Wood was one of the locations to which people gravitated for recreation at weekends and at holiday times, from Easter onwards each year. Dean Wood also had economic importance. During the 1912 strike in the coal industry, miners used their local expertise to obtain fuel to keep their homes warm. The 'burgy' coal seam outcropped on the sides of the banks that sloped down to the brook that ran through the picturesque Dean Wood.

Men with picks and shovels used the 'long wall' system to extract the coal, throwing the dirt behind them as they worked. Their efforts exposed earlier workings and an old cobblestone roadway along the deep hollow of the wood. However, for most people Dean Wood was synonymous with natural beauty, which they appreciated by following the brook through to Gathurst where it ran into the River Douglas.

75 Sometimes visits to local beauty spots were arranged. On 25 May 1907 the Stag Angling Society held its annual tea party and fishing trip. Members met a wagonette at The Stag at 8 a.m. travelled to the Old Mill House at Rufford for a day's fishing. On their return they enjoyed a knife and fork tea and an evening of entertainment, which included music, singing and dancing. During the 1920s and 1930s, as leisure time increased, villagers became rather more adventurous travellers. Works, public houses and churches organized charabanc trips; this tour was provided for the women of Lamberhead Green Independent Methodist Church. Coach firms included Cadman's of Orrell, William Webster's and James Smith's of Wigan. Groups of working men and women ventured further afield with their children to the growing seaside resorts of Southport, Morecambe, Blackpool, New Brighton and North Wales.

76 This picture showed the construction of the Majestic Cinema in Sefton Road, which perhaps represented the zenith of leisure provision in Orrell. The contractors were Dickinson and Sons of Up Holland and it was built entirely with local materials. The new cinema was planned to accommodate five hundred people. It was opened on 16 November 1936 by Sir Samuel Brighouse, the veteran Coroner for South West Lancashire. Also present at the official opening ceremony was Mr. Gordon Macdonald, Member of Parliament for the Ince Division, in which Orrell was located for electoral purposes. The Majestic was a useful addition to the social fabric of the village. In February 1938 pupils from Holgate School attended a film lecture at the cinema on Care of the Teeth and Physical Training. Orrell's only cinema closed in March 1966 because of competition from television and a restricted supply of films. Since then the building has been used as a supermarket and by a double glazing company.